I0075046

The Real Deal For Women™ Buying Cars

How to Save Huge Amounts of Money and Negotiate Like the Professionals!

Linda Fleming Balk

The Real Deal For Women™ Series

Published by:

Bamboo Publishers Inc
PO Box 540598
Lake Worth, Fl 33467

Copyright Registration TX 6-823-937

ISBN 978-0-9797012-0-7

The Real Deal For Women™

©2007 Linda Fleming Balk. All Rights Reserved Worldwide

Limits of Liability/Disclaimer of Warranty

The authors and publisher of this book and the accompanying materials have used their best efforts in preparing this ebook/manual/book/program. The authors and publisher make no representation or warranties with respect to the accuracy, applicability, fitness, or completeness of the contents of this program. They disclaim any warranties (expressed or implied), merchantability, or fitness for any particular purpose. The authors and publisher shall in no event be held liable for any loss or any other damages, including but not limited to special, incidental, consequential or other damages. As always, the advice of a competent legal, tax, accounting or other professional should be sought. The authors and publisher do not warrant the performance, effectiveness or applicability of any sites listed in this ebook/book. All links are for information purposes only and are not warranted for content, accuracy or any other implied or explicit purpose. This manual in the form of an ebook/manual/book/program or any other media contains material protected under the International and Federal Copyright Laws and Treaties.

Any unauthorized reprint or use of this material is prohibited without the express written permission of the author.

Dedication

To my husband, Victor Balk for his devotion, and
endless kindness.

To the best parents and family anyone could ever have !

In remembrance of our wonderful friend Diane
Bumgardner, for her encouragement and friendship.
We will never forget her ready wit, her happy smile,
and her generous nature.

Why You Have to Read
The Real Deal For Women™ Buying Cars!

This book is a gold mine for women who need a dynamic solution to real world financial problems! Amazing ways are revealed to negotiate on big ticket items and uncover hidden charges you probably didn't know about.

Have you ever felt intimidated when buying a car or any major purchase? Did you ever wonder if you might have paid too much?

All the practical tools are gathered together in this simple step by step analysis of The Real Deal for Women Buying Cars. Welcome to a new world of successful negotiation!

Bamboo Publishers Inc.
PO Box 540598
Lake Worth, Fl 33454
http://www.bamboopublishers.com

Table of Contents

The Real Deal For Women™ Buying Cars

You may be among the millions of women who would choose to run laps around Texas rather than drive to a dealership to buy a car.

Women are frequently treated as though they have no more than half a brain, no money, and bad credit. They are often approached by salesmen with distain and false assumptions. They are asked to come back with their husbands or someone who knows about vehicles ("Honey!"). If they are seeking trucks, even for businesses they own, it can be difficult to get waited on at all, even when they are fully qualified for the purchase, and amazingly, even when they are more qualified financially than their male counterparts. I would be willing to bet that you have experienced these strange behaviors at one time or another on the part of salesmen or management if you have entered this marketplace.

What is interesting about this phenomenon is that it flies in the face of the fact that most women today, married or single, often have the last say in the purchase of the car or truck. Women have their own jobs, tend to guard their credit ratings, and are generally very discerning buyers.

At a recent seminar, I asked a group of women how they would feel if someone on the street grabbed their purse and ran with it. Suppose that day they were carrying a couple hundred dollars and now the money was gone along with their credit cards and identification. Everyone agreed that they would call the police, start the process of protecting their credit, and lament the loss of the two hundred dollars. Even the purse might be something special that has serious value.

Yet, every day, women can leave places like dealerships, paying hundreds or thousands more for a car than other buyers, with all that extra money gone, and no appreciable difference in the product they have received. Many believe they got a great deal and leave feeling wonderful. They just lost big money by comparison with the stolen pocket book and will even pay interest on what they lost, but no one can call the police. No crime has been committed because a contract was signed with the consent of the buyer. In all fairness, dealers own the vehicles and have every right to sell them for as much as possible.

I have wonderful news! If you read this book from top to bottom you will probably be so good at getting the best deal that you will have to get your friends to buy copies of this book so that they will stop asking you to go buy cars for them.

This book is for you, the intelligent woman who is fed up with the way things are and who wants respect and recognition for the accomplishment of earning those hard earned dollars that are being taken from you without your knowledge. I want you to have what is fair and right. If you have a daughter, make sure that she gets her own copy before she buys her first car.

By now you might be wondering who I am and what excites me so much about helping you to navigate your way to more money. I am Linda Balk, someone just like you. I worked as a sales person in a car dealership trying to make a living for myself and my two sons, after a divorce. I wound up there because I needed a job and a car simultaneously. I decided that if I sold cars, I would find out how to buy one and perhaps pick up a decent one that was being traded in.

Can you imagine being so intimidated about the prospect of buying a car that it was easier to become a car sales person than to go to a dealership as a buyer?

As a side note: The salesmen who were asked to train me on the product wouldn't cooperate, so I went to the mechanics to see if they would talk to me. They were so happy that a sales person would take the time to know all the things they loved about these vehicles that they armed me with dozens of hidden features to share with customers.

Getting the job was easy because many dealerships will hire almost anyone who is or can become a sales person. What I am sharing with you is personal experience buying and selling vehicles and saving a ton of money. I want to give you the power to get a fair deal. The publisher's name is in the front of the book, so let me hear from you. Visit http://www.realdealforwomen.com today.

Actually, while vehicle purchases are used in the following examples, the same principles apply to negotiation for just about anything. This book was written so that if you encounter any or all of the scenarios I have described, you will be fully prepared to deal with the situation.

This book must be read in it's entirety to prepare you for getting the best deal because negotiation takes place on so many levels and you need to understand all of them to be effective.

All dealerships are not alike, so I have tried to cover everything that you might encounter when you are shopping for a vehicle.

Arriving At The Dealership

Did you know that when you drive in and park your car in front of the showroom you generally are under observation even before you get out of the car? The waiting sales people have already taken recognizance and made judgments about the car you might be trading in, whether it is a two door or four door car (possibly indicating your preferences), the color you chose last time, and whether the car indicates that you are the sporty type or focused on utility.

They are in that building waiting to see how many people step out of the car and hoping that it will be a husband and wife, because the belief persists, in spite of all evidence to the contrary, that if a man is involved, there will be a better chance that he will qualify for the purchase. The woman is frequently treated as though she is simply along for the ride. If you are a woman alone, you may not realize that the boss may have actually have had to force a salesman to work with you. Among many sales people the opinions of women are considered inconsequential to the sale.

If you are looking for logic, you will not find it in this setting. I am passionate about challenging the way women are treated and together we can give you the power you deserve and that your money commands.

My vision is of a woman walking up the steps to the showroom with an army of women behind her, backing her, and proclaiming by their numbers that they know what they are doing and commanding respect for their friend. The people peering out the showroom see them and jump back because the rules have changed. We changed them. There is a new force to be reckoned with and respected. Your business and money are running the show.

The Second You Arrive Negotiations Have Begun

If you don't remember any other thing in this book remember this. You may have been taught by relatives that negotiation is sitting down at the table and arriving at a price.

Nothing could be further from the truth. Have you ever wondered why it takes so many hours to buy a car? The reason is that there is sufficient time to extract information from you prior to the meeting at the table that could give the dealership the upper hand at the time of closing the deal and arriving at a price.

When you enter those beautiful doors, you have all the power. Over the next few hours the barrage of data you are given has one purpose only, and that is to convince you on some level that you have no power. So, let's change that!

A warning! During your visit talk only about the car. You will pay more if you divulge family problems, the fact that your car died last week or is on it's last legs, any divorce or eminent divorce, any proclivity for rash spending habits, a big ego, competition with your neighbor, becoming a widow, insecurity about your knowledge of cars, or really, just about anything personal. This won't be easy the first time around because you are a friendly caring person. If you want the best deal just remember that these folks are not your friends and you will probably never see them again.

Should you bring a friend with you if you don't feel strong enough and you are single? No! Absolutely not! Let me say that again. No! Absolutely not!

Frankly, I don't even bring my husband along. I bought him his last truck and he was glad to hand me the job because he knows I sold cars and he understands the principles in this book. You see, the problem is that he has new truck fragrance in his nostrils. If he were to go to the dealership with me, this fact could be detected by the salesmen early on and render me ineffective in my mission to get the real deal.

Bringing a friend along to protect you could reveal that you are weak prey and exacerbate the idea that you are a woman who can't hold her own. Your friend will most likely give the salesmen clues and information you might not want them to have. I saw one gentleman railroad his girlfriend into the paying the sticker price of the car with no questions asked. He knew less about buying a car than most five year olds, but was there as her protector.

Another helpful gentleman encouraged his female companion to make a really bad decision. This lovely middle aged woman had a low income and a dying vehicle. She brought along her employer. He scorned the idea of buying a used car that I knew was in wonderful condition, priced right, and that she could use for years. The car only had nineteen thousand miles on it, with a potential life of 300,000 miles. She believed that he must know what he was talking about. They left and I never saw her again.

Later the same day, I bought the car that she walked away from, a 1986 wagon. It handled and sounded exactly like the new ones I was driving every day. When my customer and her employer drove away, I realized that this little car could save me a ton of money and give me a vast improvement in transportation. The previous owner was a man who believed implicitly that you have to get rid of a car every two years. He provides a public service by trading in perfectly good vehicles and taking the hit on depreciation for the rest of us.

After they left the dealership, I went to the management, purchased the car for around $6000.00 and drove it for another fifteen years. It survived two sons, who drove it all over town with their band instruments, friends, and various enterprises. When the car was around seventeen years old I still used it as leverage to buy a new car. It had no monetary value as a trade, but because it was still looking and working so well, I could honestly say that I really didn't need a car during the final negotiations. If the deal hadn't worked, I still had a car to drive. How could a dealership fight with that? **I had a get-away car.**

One last word about avoiding having a person with you while you are trying to negotiate. There are people in some cities who offer their services to negotiate for you. What do you think is going to happen if they are regular visitors at a dealership, bringing in clients and selling cars? Whose side might they really be representing?

Entering The Showroom

By now you have left your vehicle and someone might even be opening the door for you. After all, you are the customer. Your manner, stature, demeanor, and clothing have all been assessed for an evaluation of your financial status. It pays to look like you have money, because the management will give perks to people that they know can go anywhere to buy a car. So, dress well for a better deal.

You might be noticing that the showroom is just magnificent. Remember that later when someone is telling you they sell all their cars below invoice or that they just can't help you with the price you thought you could buy the car for. Where do they find the money for this palace! I think we both know.

Try not to take deep breaths in the showroom at this point. You laugh, but it is loaded with new car smell and all of your senses are brought into play. You see the shiny paint on the perfect cars, the chrome is gleaming, the upholstery is new, and even the tires are spotless. Your resolve to do things differently this time is turning to hopeless mush. Before the salesman even speaks, the trap has been set.

"So, what brings you to our dealership today?" he says politely. But he already knows. A person who begins looking for a car will usually purchase one within a few days of the time they step into the first showroom or lot.

Why? Because there is no other reason for anyone to subject themselves to the treatment they have come to expect from most car dealers. In other words, few people would ever go to a car dealership just to have fun that day, so if you are there in person, you are in the market. It doesn't matter when you reply, "We are just looking" and he says "Great!" because he has already fast forwarded to the signing of the documents and a picture of you looking back in your new rear view mirror as you drive away.

How You Can Get Ready In Advance

This book is written for women, single or married, in any walk of life. If you have a husband, you cannot assume that he knows this turf any better than yourself, so if he makes the deal by himself, you might have to be the one who ultimately has to grin and bear it, or get a third job to afford it. Rather than have a situation that calls for compromise at a later date, you need to have a conference prior to driving to the showroom. Ask yourselves, **"What are we looking for?"**.

If You Are Married or a Couple- If your other half wants a sports car, and you feel the need for a wagon, don't go to the dealership until you agree upon something that meets your mutual needs and budget. You might be the one coping with groceries, the pets, and the children and your needs have to be met to have a smooth running ship. If money is no object, this is less of a burden, but it is still important to know in advance what you both want. Salespeople can exploit the differences between you. You might feel cornered into having a car with a trunk the size of a lunchbox because of the mutual pressure of wanting to make your counterpart happy and the overwhelming sales pressure. Speak up before you are in the dealership.

If you Are Single- The choice is yours but you need to narrow down to the model you want. Why? You need to avoid being sold a more expensive model than the one you came to see. You see, all businesses have concerns about inventory. For instance, in the car business, it is possible to wind up with too many blue cars, too many four doors, or whatever, in stock. Your needs and wishes are less important to the management than their need to even out inventory or get a particular car off the lot. Once your credit report is accessed with your permission and your ability to buy is analyzed, some managers will attempt to get every one of those accessible dollars from your pocket to the companies' pocket.

I wrote this book to give you the edge, so I am asking you to resist the impulse to change your plans at the last minute and choose another vehicle. Feel free to smile and politely ask the manager if he will make up the difference in the price of the car out of his own pocket, if he is suggesting that you buy the next highest priced model, or one with more accessories. That will usually end the discussion.

There is another reason why I strongly suggest that you not shift your focus to another model. You may have studied the prices for the model you came in for. Now, you are on a different car and you really can't do the math while you are there. All of your research is null and void and you are in a state of confusion. You can only win if you leave in your own car, do the research again, and come back to do this all over again. Who would want to do that? So, know what you came to buy, do the research, and stay with your deal.

What do we need to know in advance of our trek to the dealer? My friend, you are in the middle of a calibrated machine. If you don't have an idea of the true value of the vehicle you are considering for purchase, once you are at a dealership, the price is harder to find than the North American Yeti. Even if there is an additional sticker on the car with the suggested retail price, the car may be decked out with accessories that muddy the waters of reason and befuddle the best of us.

You have to have the confidence that comes with knowing that you are absolutely right about the price before you arrive.

New Versus Used

Depending upon the economic environment and other factors there are sometimes good used cars that will take you far on a budget.

If you don't know an engine from a tree, make sure you have an independent mechanic you can trust check the car out and give you an opinion on the car's condition.

Don't let your mechanic negotiate for you or get involved in buying the car. Just because he knows the inner workings doesn't mean he ever made a good deal on anything in his life. Visit the internet and find the prices that relate to the vehicle and use the same formula for the deal as with new cars. Type in the words "car invoice" into your search bar.

What Is The Price?

Years ago dealers used to walk around with little books with all the retail and wholesale values and access to the information was limited in the public sector.

Great News! You can go online to websites with all the information you want about the invoice price on the car you want, whether it is new or used. I generally start negotiating at around $600.00 over invoice. Unfortunately, this is a starting point and there are other considerations which will be covered in this book. I will help you to deal with them.

You will need to know:

1. **Invoice Price of the new vehicle**

2. **Price of the Accessories available for this vehicle**

3. **Which accessories are Standard Equipment**

4. **Average wholesale price for a car you are trading in**

5. **Retail price of the car you are trading in**

6. **Your own credit report**

Never, Never, Never Negotiate Using A MONTHLY PAYMENT!

We need to talk about monthly payments for a moment. You might have noticed that I have been only working with the total price of the car. If you try to deal backwards from a monthly payment you will lose the deal you want around 90% of the time. I cannot tell you how many people go to a dealership and pronounce that they won't make a payment over a certain amount.

The salesman may nod, smile and assure you that he will try to make sure that the payment is within that amount. Then the person controlling the deal or your friendly finance and insurance person will find every way possible to add interest or additional years to the contract, so that yes, you get a payment sort of like the one you came for, but if you multiply the months times the interest times the payment you wanted, the price of the car can become astronomical. If this happens, the car is not worth what you are paying for it. Dollars like these could put the kids through college someday or buy better transportation. What is even worse is that the loan can be so high compared to the price of the car that if you try to trade it in at a later date, you could find yourself in a bad situation with the loan amount exceeding the value of the car. Guess what will happen to the difference? If you don't come up with cash to make up the difference, it will be added to the loan on you **next** car, and the cycle of automobile impoverishment continues for another few years. I am counting on you to stop this cycle and start owning your own money.

Go and buy a little book called an amortization table or get one off the internet. You should at the very least have a calculator or a loan calculator. Take it with you to the dealership so that you can take a look at what the monthly payment would be if the price of the car is for example, $20,000.00 at an interest rate of 4% for a term of 48 months. You will know the amount of the monthly payment and you will be sure that the payment is correct, relative to the price negotiated, the interest rate and the term.

If you don't know these numbers you have no power and you are toast (meaning you have as much power as a piece of toast). In the shuffle of numbers you could get a fair price on the car and lose some or all your equity in the car you are trading in. If you do well negotiating the price of the car and the trade, you could be offered an interest rate or term of the loan, that will again lose some of what you have gained.

What else should I know in advance? Get some idea what prevailing interest rates are by going to a bank and checking generally on the rates being offered on car loans. Check your credit union. Check everywhere. If you have a good relationship with your banker, you might be able to get a better rate than the one offered by the dealership.

Also, don't forget that you can usually refinance a car after you buy it if the rates are more advantageous elsewhere. If you want to do this, do it as soon as possible, because your new car is already depreciating in value when you drive it off the lot.

People who pay cash for the car don't necessarily get a better deal on vehicles. Surprised? Dealerships make a lot of their income from dealing with companies that finance your loan and some might do the financing themselves. If you pay cash, they make less money in the long run, so they will try very hard to get the highest possible price for the car if they aren't involved in procuring your financing. If you are paying cash, never discuss the fact until you have made the deal on the car.

Try to think of negotiating the price as a separate process from negotiating the interest rates. Everything depends on what the prevailing interest rates are at the time you buy. If you are offered a 1% rate on your purchase for the life of the loan, why would you bother with a hefty down payment? On the other hand, if you had a credit problem and were told the interest rate is 12%, you have a major problem that can be solved with a cash down payment to lower the total you have to pay back. You might have to start thinking about a less expensive car or keep what you have for a while. Also, if your credit can be repaired or a mistake is on your report, do what it takes to get it corrected before you arrive to negotiate on a car.

I have to interject a word of caution here. Because of the widespread use of home equity lines, I am hearing people talk about using them for cars because of the lower interest rate. I do not recommend using this source for a vehicle because what you gain in the interest rate, you lose on the term of the loan. You could also jeopardize the ownership of your home if you are unable to pay back the loan. In any case you are decreasing your equity in your most valuable asset. **Depending upon your age, your retirement could also be affected.** For the sake of your financial well-being, find another way. Sometimes a relative has a car they could sell you or if you are over 65, in some parts of the country, public transportation is a phone call away. Find a way to keep your money. Consider buying from a private party. What would it cost to take a cab?

Buying From a Private Party

When my youngest son, Scott was nearing the age when he could drive I was able to help him using the principles in this book. To this day, I am very grateful because helping him find his first car was something we could work on together, at a time when teenage sons are rather hard to connect with. Our first jaunt was to the Sheriff's office auction. We looked over what they had that day and decided to bid on a small car that in my opinion should sell for no more than $1200.00. Mind you, we couldn't drive these cars, but there wasn't much risk if the price was low enough.

The auctioneer was on his way, people got caught up in the competition (a very bad way to buy)! We dropped out at our maximum bid and watched when the auctioneer said, "and the winner is…" I whispered to my son, "He is a winner alright! Wait until he finds out he spent $3500.00 on a wholesale car he could get anywhere for around $1200.00 or less! Let's get some lunch!" That day, Scott started walking away from bad deals and not looking back. I was proud of the way he took it in stride.

We then started looking at the cars he found in the newspaper and I taught him to sight down the side of the cars to look for differences in the paint. When you can detect a difference in the paint it can indicate body work on the vehicle. An event or accident may have occurred that could make the car less than desirable. After a while, he could pick out incongruities faster than I could and ask the right questions. I had his respect, which was all I cared about at the time.

Finally, we went to the home of a very nice family selling a car that their daughter would not be taking to a distant college. They told us they were selling it because the insurance was so expensive. We drove the car and it turned out to be solid on the road, but we knew it needed repairs. They were asking $2700.00 and I asked Scott to please let me do the talking and stop looking eager. He really wanted this one.

I asked the husband and wife to realize that Scott had been saving money for a car and didn't have nearly what they hoped to sell the car for. We didn't want to make it difficult for them, but were constrained to a budget of around $700.00 because the car needed a brake service and other work. I explained that Scott would have to handle the insurance bill and do repairs as he made money in order to buy the car. I let them know that overall it was the nicest used car we had seen.

We told them that Scott was willing to transfer the car and pay cash right away so that they could cancel their insurance immediately. We asked them to think about it that night and asked if it would be alright to call the next day. Every step of the way we let them know we would respect whatever decision they made.

The wife walked off with her husband and they talked quietly for a minute. When they came back, they said they would like to go ahead and sell the car to Scott. We thanked them and came back the next day, insured and ready to transfer the title.

When we were on the way home, Scott was very quiet and asked me "How did you do that? They wanted $2700.00 and they could have gotten it." I will never forget the look of admiration on his face. I told him that there was no secret. They wanted out of the car and out of the insurance. It was dead weight and they didn't want to make the repairs and keep the car. But the most important thing was that we had simply explained our position and asked them to consider what we were saying. We made it easy for them to make a decision because we were peaceful and truthful that it was a great little car.

It was a sporty car with all the bells and whistles. Scott drove it for years after making about 1200.00 worth of repairs. He worked at a restaurant to pay for everything and bought it before he was old enough to drive (it was in my name for a while). He made his repairs and waited for his sixteenth birthday. Do you think I had to worry that he would be irresponsible with that car? Not for a second.

If you buy a privately owned vehicle, just be straight about what you can do. Realize that people are sometimes emotionally attached to vehicles and want them to go to people they like. Be quiet, peaceful, and thoughtful. If you need a mechanics opinion on the condition, have him come to the home and take a look, but let him know that you want his opinion in private, not in front of the owner.

Pay him something for his time, because you might have to repeat the process and his services are not costly compared to making a mistake.

You will have to be able to pay a lump sum, because people usually will not carry payments. Make it easy for them and they will make it easy for you.

The Power of Positioning

What do I mean by positioning? You will see this in other chapters of the Real Deal For Women.

Positioning, for the purpose of getting the best price, is the way and means you have developed for yourself which enable you to get the optimum value for your money. Positioning can help you whether you are wealthy or not wealthy and give you power over what appear to be insurmountable odds.

So, let's talk about positioning as it relates to buying a car.

Have you checked your credit score? The folks at the dealership will have to pull (get access to) your credit score and payment habits to even consider selling you a car. If your credit score is good and you are known to pay your bills on time, even if you don't make a lot of money, you can still be eligible to buy a car. The higher the credit score, the better you are positioned to negotiate because they know that you can buy a car anywhere. You can get the deal you want because you are dealing from strength.

If you have a great credit rating, but don't *know* how good it is, you are not positioned well, and could be led to believe that you don't have any power. So, before you go to the dealership, know where you stand.

Is your present vehicle still running? Have you ever known someone who pushed a car so far that by the time they were ready to drive to a dealership, it was dead? Now the trade-in car is gone, a tow truck has to be paid to take the car to the dump, and the car salesman knows that you need a way to get to work. You have not positioned yourself to get the right price because it is hard to radiate confidence when you perceive yourself as defeated. Don't let your car die before you shop for a new one. If it is too late for this advice, come up with a plausible alternative like your Mother is thinking of giving you her car, or something, to get your power back and maximize your positioning.

Did you arrive at the dealership looking like a queen or did you walk in looking like an unmade bed today? Dress up and position yourself as an independent, smart woman, who will not be intimidated. Remember, we are all behind you! People who look powerful usually are. Your salesman is reading what you look like, so look fantastic.

Are you determined to use the principles in this book? If you believe the contents, it could still be hard for you to follow through and actually use the material you have been given. I am asking you to come with me and get what you deserve. If you don't feel powerful yet, just believe that you are, and give it your best. You will be so surprised by the outcome!

Are you brain washed into believing you have to trade a car in every three years or so? The biggest proponents of this notion are employed by car dealerships. They want you to pay top dollar for a new car and take the big hit for depreciation in the first few years. Then they want you to give it back to them soon to sell to another person for a price you probably wouldn't believe, compared to what they gave you.

What a lot of people don't realize is that car technology has made the average vehicle last a very long time with very few problems if the car is properly maintained. Why would you continue a pattern that erodes your wealth and make car dealers rich? Find out what the average life of your car can be, maintain it according to schedule, and drive it as long as you can. The money you save can be used to invest and grow more money.

A car is not an investment. You may have heard people talk about a car as an investment. An investment is made to make your money make more money. When has a car ever made you money? Even if you write off expenses for a business for income taxes, you don't get to keep the money. You only get to pay less taxes at the end of the year because the deductions reduce your income. That amount could just be a fraction of the cost of the vehicle.

Cars cost you money. They depreciate until they have no value. They rust and turn to dust. Unless you have a fortune and don't care about money (although people who have fortunes **do** care about money most of the time) don't throw away money on something that is not an investment. This is useful information if your salesman suggests that you should invest in a car. You will be positioned to make a good choice. Challenge this and ask with enthusiasm, "So this car is going to give me income? I can't wait to get my first check! When will I get it?"

Don't call me honey! Hold your head high and position yourself to handle deprecating remarks with aplomb. How are you going to negotiate if you allow people to talk down to you? At the first sign of this, speak up politely and assert that you prefer to be called by whatever name you choose. If you feel like you are dealing with piranhas (normally found in the Amazon), mention that you aren't just buying a car, you are buying a dealership. The way you are treated will determine where you spend your money and you are very sensitive about being talked down to. You won't believe how fast piranhas can back paddle.

By the way, I have been asked many times whether women in the car business are more honest than the men. My personal opinion, and you are free to disagree with me, is that it doesn't matter because ultimately your salesperson is not going to have any control over the price of the car. That decision will come from the management.

Positioning has more to do with your true belief system than with the reality of any situation. If you have to practice your lines in the mirror, it will be worth the effort. Think of yourself as a highly paid actress playing the part of a powerful buyer.

The Danger of Co-Signing
For a Loan

Has someone you love asked you to co-sign on a loan? I can't begin to tell you how many times I have heard horror stories from women who decided to help a friend, child, or relative. Perhaps the person's credit was not sufficient to get a loan on a car. So, these women became co-signers on a loan to help them out.

What a lot of them failed to understand was that if the person they were helping ever defaulted on the loan, missed payments, or was routinely late, it would reflect directly on the co-signer's credit report. A person who co-signs on a loan is totally responsible for the loan as much as the person they tried to help out.

Women who have been nurturing people all their lives find it almost impossible to say no in a situation like this. If you are one of these women, I am asking you to take charge and let other people get their own loans without your participation. Your best and perhaps only defense is to stay out of the problem by not physically going to the dealership.

How would you feel if you couldn't buy a car yourself, because someone you co-signed for has ruined your good credit by reneging on a loan. Your credit score might not be sufficient to get a car that you need to get to work. It can affect all of your financial dealings if a negative entry shows up on your credit report. The best way to stay out of the co-signer role is just simply to stay out of the dealership. Refuse to go there with the person who is asking for your help. It is too easy for nurturing women to get pulled into the wishes of other people and sign on the dotted line as a co-buyer, surrounded by the salesman, the car, and the friend.

Another result of co-signing on a loan could be that if you need additional credit for yourself, you could be denied a higher credit limit on other loans or credit cards. Lending institutions will count the co-signed loan against your income and might perceive you to be over-extended. This can happen even if the person you co-signed for is paying everything right on time and causing no problems.

Heaven forbid that the person you co-signed for allows the car to be repossessed. Do you want to take a chance that your name is attached to that car?

Timing Gives You Power

Choose a good time of day for yourself, like after breakfast or lunch when you are at your best. Negotiation is going to take you around four to five hours to accomplish, so give yourself time. Choose the portion of the day when you have focus and clarity of mind.

Buy at the end of the month-People have asked me for years whether it is true that it is better to buy a car on the last day of the month. My opinion is yes.

It is no secret that the managers in dealerships have pressurized quotas for the number of cars they need to get off the lot. In general, each of the cars on the lot is taking up space by the day, which is an expense to the dealership. The longer they stay, the more expensive they are to the establishment.

By the end of the month, time is running out to get those extra cars off the lot and hopefully, parked in **your** garage. So, feel free to shop for the best deal when the pressure is on management to move cars.

If You Can, Buy in December- I bought my last car and my husband's truck on the last day of the year, December 31. Why? December, because of the holidays and travel plans is usually not a time when people want to bother with buying cars. Dealership floors tend to look empty, sales are frequently in the doldrums, and your presence there is coveted. You are in a better position when things are slow. Besides, the manager is not only dealing with month end figures, but year end accounting.

What Am I Buying?

Spend a significant amount of time exploring this question. **A lot of people think that they are buying a car.** Right? Any car or vehicle salesman will tell you that nothing is further from the truth. They know that a lot of people come to buy something like this:

- ❖ A Way To Get More Dates

- ❖ A Statement About Who You Are

- ❖ A Way To Get Noticed

- ❖ A Way To Impress Friends

- ❖ Transportation To And From Work

- ❖ A Traveling Machine

- ❖ A Car That Will Live In Two States

- ❖ The Penultimate Sound System

- ❖ The Fountain Of Youth

- ❖ A Home Away From Home

- ❖ A Child Mobile

- ❖ Popularity With The Other Moms

- ❖ A Workhorse

- ❖ Recognition Of Success

- ❖ Acceptance Of Peers

- ❖ A Way To Conquer Any Turf

- ❖ Admiration Of Friends

- ❖ A Way to Impress Relatives

- ❖ A Financial Statement

- ❖ A Way To Feel Happy

❖ Showing Up An Ex-Spouse

❖ Protection For Your Child

These are just a few of the traps you can fall into. You can wind up spending money for something you never intended to buy for a price you could have started an annuity with. I would like to define what I believe a car really is.

A car is a machine made of many parts that will convey a person from point A to point B.

I can get anywhere as easily and as fast in my economical car as a billionaire can in a limo. You can only drive the speed limit, so what does it matter if a car can go 200 mph in 60 seconds. Do you really need four wheel drive in Miami, where the highest altitude you can drive to is in a parking garage? Will you really get more dates in a convertible?

Learn Everything About The Car

If your salesman sort of waves at the car and wants to know what you want to do, get another salesman. A good salesman should lift the hood and take you through the engine, to the interior of the car and on to the inside of the storage sections so that you will know what you are buying. Clarify the safety features, upholstery, etc. You should have a chance to ask questions about the car, the existing warranty, any dealer promotions that are running, and the availability of the color you want.

Don't let anyone rush you. You have set aside time, driven to the showroom, and they are going to keep you busy for the next few hours anyway. Remember, you have already started the negotiation process and you have to maintain control of the situation to get the deal you came for.

In the showroom, sit down in the front seat for a few minutes and get the feel of the contours and the seat levels to see if the car is going to be comfortable over a long period of time. There is nothing worse than finding out on a long trip that your back is aching, you feel like you are pushing the whole car down the road with your right foot, or that you have a headache from the glare off of a giant dashboard.

Ask about the frequency of maintenance, the cost of maintenance and the expected mileage. A gas hog can break your bank down the road. What kind of tires come with the car? How many miles can you expect out of them before you have to buy new ones?

Can you see out well or do you feel like the visibility is inhibited in some way. Maybe for a taller person this would be a great car, but for you, it feels like you are inside an army tank.

Review what the car comes with, versus added on accessories. The question to ask is:

What is standard equipment?

STANDARD EQUIPMENT

As we discussed, the price of the car can be a moving target if you don't know what the car comes with at the invoice price.

You see, the invoice price you found on the internet includes all the accessories that come as standard equipment. If the car has something like a DVD player that is not standard equipment, and it is already installed in the car, the dealer might assign a value to it that is much higher than you would expect to find in a retail store. So, if you aren't ready for this, you could pay vastly more than the ordinary price for an accessory (just because it is already installed in the car you are buying!) and then **pay interest** on it for the next few years too.

There is a powerful alternative. **Buy the vehicle with only the standard equipment. If they tell you an expensive accessory is already on the car, tell them to remove it.** If they won't comply, let them know you are leaving the dealership, politely thank them for their time, and physically head for your vehicle. You might be surprised to find that they won't let you leave after all, and that suddenly everything becomes possible.

Let them know that you will wait for a car to arrive from the manufacturer without the add-ons and to call you when it arrives, remove the add-on, or lower the price of the add-on.

Why pay interest for years on a special radio? You can buy it for cash at a better price and have it installed later. It doesn't become part of a car loan. Keep your money in your pocket and get the same product and satisfaction.

THE TEST DRIVE

So far, you've done a great job and followed the instructions in the book. I want you to get behind the wheel and see how the car handles and whether it is really what you want. If you buy a car without driving it, you could be making a huge mistake that you will regret every time you have to go anywhere. It is not a bad idea to test drive the car a day ahead of making the deal on it. You need to be sure of your selection and complete your research on the car.

Your salesman will probably drive you out of the dealership and navigate you to a quiet neighborhood where he won't be in much peril with you behind the wheel. He will also try to put you in an upscale environment where everything is neat and lovely, because you will be glad that you are in this location in your new car, instead of your old one. Your salesman wants you to take possession of this vehicle and consider it your own. He wants you to bond with the car.

Did you know that your salesman might wait to ask some key questions for the moment you are behind the wheel? This is just a personal observation, but I have

noticed over the years that it is very difficult to deflect a direct question when you are driving.

I believe the reason is that you are concentrating on the road and questions become a secondary thing for you to handle. Because of this you will tend to answer a direct question with the first thing you come up with, the whole truth, in an instant. This can work against you in later negotiations.

Just a note: I once used this principle to find out the identity of a person that a business partner had hired. Every time I asked about the new recruit I got an evasive answer regarding why he was among us. We were struggling with payroll at the time and I wanted answers.

I waited until he was driving and asked him directly why this new person was in our midst and if he was somehow related to him. He answered that the young man was his ex-girlfriend's son, that he owed her money and that by giving her son a job, he was paying her off. Then he looked at me like he couldn't believe he had just blurted out the truth. The recruit and the partnership were soon severed.

Suppose you are a single woman on the test drive. Your salesman might ask you if you like the way the car handles. You might reply that it is certainly better than the car you own. So, he knows that this is definitely a plus. No harm is done to your negotiation positioning because you haven't revealed much personal data.

Now suppose that out of the blue, he asks if this car will make your trip to work more pleasant. You are concentrating on the road and you might shoot back "It really would because I am a field representative and spend a lot of time in my car going to see customers." "No kidding", he says, "What company are you with?" You reply that you are with a large national retailer.

He now has a tremendous edge during negotiations because he knows you are the only buyer that he has to deal with, you are ready for more comfort, and perhaps more prestige. You have a sales presence and your customers might see you in your car. You probably make above average income. He also knows that you have a busy schedule, your time is limited and you probably want to just get it over with. Therefore, the dealership has information that will make it possible to aggressively attempt to get more money out of you and complete the deal today.

To get the deal you came for:

1. Keep the test drive a reasonable length of around 25-30 minutes.

2. Before you answer anything, pause for a few seconds, think it through, and carefully phrase your response.

3. Avoid answering a lot of questions while you are driving.

4. Ask your salesman about the car or dealership.

Back At the Dealership

You have arrived back at the dealership and parked the car. It is possible that your salesman will offer to check the inventory to see if the car is available.

You might shriek, "What do you mean, I told you this is the car I am interested in." So, he knows you are hooked on this particular car and asks you to come inside and work on the numbers, while he checks inventory. He might come back with the wonderful news that the car is available, but they only have one. Now an element of urgency has manifested itself.

The message is, "You had better get it or it will be gone."

I Have Great News! There Are More Being Manufactured Every day! You Can Still Get One!

You might be in a cubicle on the sales floor or in a glassed-in office. As in most businesses, managers keep a close eye on their sales people to see how they are progressing and what they are doing. Your body language and speech patterns can give away signals that you are losing your resolve to see your deal through to your satisfaction. If you say you are sure what you are paying for this car and your body language shows that you aren't relaxed and sure of yourself, you are on the way to losing your negotiating position.

Stay relaxed and comfortable. Remember that this is your money and that you don't have to do anything at all today or any day. If an agreement can be reached that is wonderful, but if it can't you will go somewhere else. You have the right to spend your money where people will work with you.

You are finally ready to discuss the price of the car. The salesman begins pecking away at a calculator like a statistician, adds up the damages, and shows you the total cost of the car. Like the price is an absolute. He asks casually if you are trading in your vehicle.

Keep the trade out of the deal or you can become lost on the cost of the new car. At this point, tell him you haven't decided what you are doing with your car and that you only want to concentrate on the price of the car you are buying.

You are getting sleepy, laced with discomfort. After all, you have just read a book about this, but what if you can't pull it off. What if they laugh at you? What if they ask you to leave?

Relax. They want to sell a car. They don't want you to leave. Pretend that you have a hide like an alligator. This is your money and your life. You have the power. Repeat to yourself, "It is my money, it is my money".

TAKE THE NEXT STEP

It is your turn to present what you think is a fair deal. Tell the salesman about your research. You know the invoice price of the car and are willing to pay whatever you feel is fair (I offered $600.00 over invoice on the last three vehicles I purchased) over that amount as a profit to the dealer. In addition, you will not pay inflated prices for any accessories that come with the car as non-standard equipment. You understand that dealerships get incentives below invoice for the number of cars they deliver (sell) in a month and that you believe that this is fair to both sides. Did you catch what I just said? High volume dealerships might possibly pay less than invoice prices for the car because manufacturers can give rewards for the volume a dealership is selling.

- ❖ Be Polite

- ❖ Be Prepared

- ❖ Be Firm

- ❖ Be Fair to Yourself

- ❖ Do not be Confrontational

❖ Don't show Anger

❖ Deal from Strength

At this point, the person across the table from you should be looking a little dazed (but some have a hide like an alligator too and might smirk). Because you have been so businesslike and polite, he might not know what to do with you, except to tell you that no car has ever been sold for that price.

Start Thinking That You Are Listening to a Quacking Duck And Pay No Attention to the Words.

One thing that I would like to stress to women is that it is easy to become outraged at the manner, tone, and posturing of salesmen. I have been on the wrong end of a sneer more than once myself. You may have become super sensitive to this kind of behavior in the past. You may have a razor tongue and a sharp wit and want to use it on them.

If you want to win, you have to put all that away and become the soul of serenity and kindness. If you become aggressive in speech or tone, they will win and have you apologizing too. In the end, it's about the money and I want the money to be yours.

Repeat your points every time someone tries to convince you that you don't know what you are talking about:

❖ I have Good Credit

❖ I have done heavy research

❖ I know the numbers

❖ My facts are correct

❖ I can buy this car anywhere.

It is now time to take a deep breath of new car fragrance and go into the battle for your own money. Smile and mention that you had really hoped to be able to do business with this particular dealership because they were highly recommended and they are close to your house, or something that sounds reasonable. You can understand that they might not do as much volume as some of the other dealerships in the area. Then, don't say anything else and don't get up out of your chair.

Your salesman now has to go to the manager and present what is happening in his cubicle. He may reach for the phone and it may seem like he is talking to the head of a major car company in a foreign country to discuss what you want. The manager is rarely more than thirty feet away and will usually call the salesman in for a conference to find out what he knows about you. Now all the details learned during the prior hours will be revisited to find any compelling reason why you might not be so strong in your convictions.

Finally, the salesman might come back and suggest that they have done everything they can, but this is a very popular model, they don't have many of these, and the manager said they just can't take more than $500.00 off the price of the car.

Please note that you were just told a short time before that the price was an absolute. Start smiling more.

Begin repeating your message. Calmly address the gentleman before you as if you are a queen, of noble ancestry, and thank him for his time today. You have been very impressed with the car and truly want to buy it, but have decided what you will pay, either at this dealership or another. The price you will pay is a total of Blah, Blah, Blah, and you want to be fair, but simply will not put that much money into the car.

Be obnoxious in a nice way and waste as much of their time as they are wasting yours, but be wonderfully polite. For instance, ask to go for another test drive or act like you might be changing your mind about the color, upholstery, or anything. Keep looking in your amortization book and pulling numbers out.

Keep mentioning that you can't work with the numbers they are presenting and will have to come back another day or go to another dealership (by the way, take a second to look up the name of their nearest competitor, and make sure they don't own both dealerships).

Change Models or Makes: Let them know that while you like this car, you also have developed a fondness for a car of an entirely different brand and perhaps should look at that one too.

You are creating the beginning of a very bad situation for the salesman, the manager, and the

dealership. Only so many customers will arrive today. It is very important to get as many cars delivered as possible. Precious time has been spent with you and it is important that you buy the car here or all the time spent with you is wasted.

Dealerships are strange places and the people who run them can have bad cases of short term memory. If a manager has had a bad week or day, you will get what you want in less time, maybe 4 hours. Sometimes, if they have had a couple of outstanding weeks, they get cocky and will allow a real customer to leave the dealership thinking the deal can't be done, only to call a couple of days later at home with the deal they could have done at any time. Hopefully, you can let them know you already bought the car elsewhere.

The only thing for sure is that you have to stick to your research and ride out the negotiations until you get what you want. You will not get what you want unless you are actually willing to walk away from the deal entirely.

Tactics used to get your dollars:
- ❖ **Intimidation**
- ❖ **Humor**
- ❖ **Sympathy**
- ❖ **Camaraderie**

At some point, the manager or another salesman will usually join you to sit down and talk things over. The belief is that if you are offered a new face to deal with, you might be more apt to work with the new person. Why? Because it is recognized in these places that you might just have a personality conflict or not like your salesman. To keep from losing any precious customer, you will be given the opportunity to speak with someone else before you will be allowed to leave without a new car.

With your permission, they have checked your credit and know whether you are someone who can qualify to buy a car. If you are a qualified customer, they want you to leave in their car. The manager will be polite and go over the numbers or he might sneer too. He will have to make a decision regarding the price of the car. **Don't bring your trade into the deal until you have established the price you are paying for the new or used vehicle you want to purchase.**

When you are at the number you offered or very close to the number your research has led you to, you can shake hands on that part and thank them for working with you. If your offer is not accepted, stand up to go. That is the only way they can recognize you are serious, that you will actually terminate the discussion if you don't get what you want. You have to be prepared to walk away from the deal and show that you are not a weak person.

❖ **Now, and only now, bring in the subject of the trade.**

What's the Deal On The Trade-In

The car you are trading in is actually a more complex issue to deal with than the one you are buying. Unlike a new car, it has a history and how it has been maintained, whether it has been in an accident, body work, interior condition, and all sorts of issues can contribute to exactly what it is worth.

However, if you can stand back and be objective, you will get some very good guidelines regarding the wholesale value of your car from the internet. If you can sell the car for cash you might get a better price dealing with the general public. This is always an option.

Why don't more people put an ad in the paper and sell their own cars? Because it is easier to get rid of the old one at the same time you buy the new one.

Women have an extra problem and the people at dealerships are aware of it. If you advertise your car and someone you don't know comes to your door to test drive the car, you could be in a dangerous position. What if this person is a car thief or worse, passes bad checks on a daily basis, or just wants to case your house for a future robbery?

Unless you are selling the car to someone you know, like a neighbor, it might be a good idea to use the principles in this book to get what you want in a safe environment.

So, knowing the approximate value of the trade-in car will help you to determine if you are being treated fairly and whether to trade the car in or sell it privately. Dealerships will only pay the wholesale value of the car, because they have to turn it around and sell it in a short time. They also might have to pay for damage to be repaired to the body or for new parts. You have to be objective about your good old car and assess the value according to the real condition of the car.

Take some time to clean and wax your vehicle before trading it in. The small amount of time you spend could get you more money.

After a certain number of years, your car has no resale value at all. A car with no book value is usually sold for a very tiny price to one of the buy here pay here lots down the street. But such a car can still serve you well as a get away car, in the event you need to let people know that you still have transportation and don't need their car at all.

❖ What to do if you are upside down

If you owe more money on your car than what the car is worth, they will tell you that you are upside down. What they mean is that in order to pay off the loan on your car you will have to pay the difference between what they are paying you for the trade-in car and the loan that you still owe on it. You will find yourself in an adverse position.

The money to make up the difference will have to come from you. If you decide to move ahead with this deal, you will have to come up with the cash to cover the difference. If you don't have the cash, the difference will be tacked on to the price of the new car, causing you to have a higher loan for the new car. I would advise you to back away from doing this because it leads to years of continued overpayment for your transportation.

I strongly advise that if you owe more on the car than the car is worth, that you continue paying the car off until the value of the car is at least equal to the amount on the loan. That way, you can at least break even on the trade-in and start fresh with the new car purchased at the right price.

Ideally, if the trade in car is completely paid for and still has a wholesale value, that entire wholesale value can be subtracted from the price you have already negotiated for the car you are buying. That makes the great price you negotiated even better.

Finance and Insurance

You could be in your fourth hour at the dealership and think you are finished with negotiating. I congratulate you for reading this book and working to get the best deal possible. I know you have done a great job so far!

You are tired and happy because you have the car you want at the price you want. **Right?**

Not yet. It is now time to be introduced to another office and another gentleman or woman, your finance and insurance person.   In general, you couldn't meet a more personable person. These folks are chosen for their passion for the numbers and stage presence.

They meet all the customers, so their time is limited. To speed things up, they talk a little faster and sometimes will tap a pencil or pen while you are trying to think. You might take the message to mean "hurry up, hurry up, hurry up, we don't have time for thinking around here".

This is a great time to slow things down. Was anyone in a hurry to do anything during the last few hours? Why should you feel any need to progress at any other than your own pace?

Finance and insurance departments are in many ways as much or more of a money making arm of the dealership as the car sales department, and I urge you to respect their power and have more power.

Why does the car dealership have people in place to offer on the spot loans, insurance, extended warranties, etc.? Dealerships make money on your loan, insurance, and extended warranties.

The good thing is that if you can qualify in any way for a car, even if you have difficult credit or other issues, they might have a lender behind them who will get you a loan, quicker and easier than your average dear banker.

But let's assume for a moment that you have pretty good credit score, which you know because you checked before you left home.

If you are uncomfortable about the interest rate, term of a loan, products, or anything about the offering, stop all the action on the car and let them know that you will not take this car today unless your concerns are addressed.

❖ **You have to be able to leave without the car today or you have no power.**

Ask about the best interest rate that can be offered by the dealership. Let them know you have other sources of financing. You can leave the dealership in your own car and shop for a better interest rate at a bank. This gives you an additional control factor, because they haven't sold your car while you are looking around.

Alternatively, you can request the right to shop for a few days for a better rate elsewhere, while driving the new car. **Just make sure your right to replace their loan with a new one within a specified number of days is noted on the contract for purchase in writing and that no penalties will be paid if you find financing elsewhere. Ask the finance person to sign or initial that phrase.**

One drawback you have is that if you are not able to get a better rate, the dealership will have sold your trade-in, so you are stuck with the deal you have. I only suggest this method if you know your credit is so strong that you can get a better deal. Don't be shy about anything that you ask.

I will share a story about the car I am still driving. The last time I purchased a car, I was presented with an interest rate that I considered too high. I thanked them for their time and rose to leave (I had worked with them for 4 hours already). They called the salesman who came charging up to take me to my car in a golf cart. My good old car was only a hundred feet away (such drama!).

On the way, he got on the phone with the manager again and they offered to give me more money for my trade-in to help defray the cost of the higher interest rate. Now the joke is that the car I was trading in had absolutely no value, it was seventeen years old! I told him that I would take the deal he was offering me on one condition, that I would be allowed to obtain a better interest rate and replace the loan within 5 days with no penalty. I completed the deal and drove my new car to two banks.

I filled out two loan applications, which triggered inquiries from the banks on my credit report. I speculated that the guys at the dealership would pull my credit report to see if I was actually out there trying to get better financing. A couple of days later, before the banks even responded, I got a call that went like this:

"Mrs. Balk, the most wonderful thing has happened. We have a new vendor who is able to reduce the interest rate we quoted you by four percent. All you have to do is come in and re-sign the paperwork." I went in and carefully reviewed the paperwork to be sure that no other changes had been made, signed the paperwork and came out of the place four percent richer on the loan. I still got to keep the extra money they gave me to defray the expense of the interest too. I paid off the car early and saved even more. The car came with a 10 year standard warranty, tires for life, and a 5 year road service at no extra cost. One of the bankers I went to told me that she had never seen anyone come in with a price so low on that car. The dealer beat the rates the banks offered me, and knew what they had to beat.

Remember that the finance officer has numerous lenders at his disposal and depending upon the relationships with those vendors may be trying to get more volume with a particular institution. Your welfare might not be the guiding star in his choice of lenders and corresponding interest rates. You have to be ready to take care of yourself in this department.

TERM

If you get everything else right and get the term of the loan on your new car wrong, you can lose almost all of your gains. Let's look at how term can affect the total price of the car you are buying.

Let's look at three total payments created by the term of the loan with all other factors being equal.

1. $20,000.00 X   3 yrs (36 Months) @ 6% = 608.44/mo

2. $20,000.00 X   4 yrs (48 Months) @ 6% = 469.70/mo

3. $20,000.00 X   5 yrs (60 Months) @ 6% = 386.66/mo

Effect on the total price:

1. 36 months X 608.44 = 21,903.84 Total Price Paid

   Total Interest Paid = 1,903.84

2. 48 Months X 469.70 = 22545.60 Total Price Paid

   Total Interest Paid = 2545.60

3. 60 Months X 386.66 = 23199.60

   Total Interest Paid = 3199.60

In this example, the person who took financing for 60 months added a total of **$3,199.60** to the original price of the car.

This is why that wonderful little amortization table book can be a priceless resource. You will know what you are paying and take control of how you want to spend your money.

❖ **So, if you pay cash you don't pay any interest, right?**

This is correct, but be aware that you are going to really have to know the right price for the car or the dealership will try to make up the difference somewhere else.

If you are going to pay cash, don't mention it until you have negotiated the price of the car, including the trade-in values.

Taxes

The total taxes added to your car contract will be based upon the price you negotiate, making that price all the more important. The less you pay for the car, the less you pay in taxes. Your tax bill will also depend upon where you live and current legislation.

Do you really want to pay **interest** on *taxes* for the term of your loan? Even if you get a loan with the lowest interest rate possible in the world, I would urge you to at least make a down payment that will pay for all of the taxes on the car.

Extended Warranties and Insurance

By now, you are being asked to think about extended warranties. These warranties are often additional warranties to the standard warranty that comes with the car. Ask your finance person if there is any **overlap** on the policies.

What I mean by this is that the car may come with a three year warranty from the manufacturer at no extra cost. If you purchased another warranty for three years, depending on the product, you need to know if it starts at the end of the other warranty or whether it will overlap an existing standard warranty. If it overlaps a year that is already covered, you are wasting money because the car was already covered and you are paying for two policies that overlap each other

Ask about exclusions in the policy and read them. You might find out the there are exclusions and limitations to coverage so dense that it would be harder to get the insurer to pay off on much of anything than it would be to ride a roller coaster standing on your head with no handlebars. On the other hand, the policy could be something with real merit. In the end, only you can decide this.

Your finance person is probably very busy tapping that pen right now and will want you out of the office, so ask if you have to take the warranty now or whether you can read it at home so you'll know what you are buying. Ask how long you have to cancel the warranty or other insurance products after buying the car, if you change your mind. Based upon the answers, try to make the best decision you can. Then, close the deal on the car if everything is the way you want it. If you are confused, uncomfortable or being rushed, leave without the car.

Anything you add on will cost you additional interest over the term of the loan. **Make sure what the rules are for canceling the warranty and how many days you have to exercise your rights without any penalties if you buy it as part of the car purchase.**

In many states there is no grace period or cancellation of a purchase contract for a car. Make sure you understand the laws in your state.

❖ Protecting Yourself with Insurance

The warranties and insurance sold in a dealership are generally not the type of insurance sold by your local property and casualty insurance agent to satisfy your State Insurance or Financial Services Department Laws.

The rules differ from state to state. I don't advise driving your new car out of the dealership without calling your insurance agent and letting them know that you have a new car and to add it to your policy, even if you have the right to more time by law. You might forget to call later. If you get into an accident, you could be denied coverage, or have coverage limited in some way. Rules differ according to state laws, so know the rules. It is just easier to call your agent from the dealership and take care of this so you won't forget.

If this is your first car, shop for insurance before you get the car and call your agent from the dealership. Shopping for insurance in advance can sometimes help you decide which car to buy. Some cars are so expensive to insure that your car payment will be the least of your worries.

I once showed a young man a used sports car. He wanted the car very badly, but I suggested that he check on the price of insurance at his age, for that particular car before making a decision. I also asked him to call a mechanic and find out about the cost of regular maintenance on the vehicle. He left and called me later that day with the news that the insurance alone would have cost him over $3000.00 a year. Needless to say, he started looking at different models.

As a first time buyer, with no existing policy, have someone from the dealership drive the new car to the insurance agent, let them bind coverage and inspect your new vehicle. If **you** drive it to the insurance agent's office, you might not be covered in the event of an accident to your new car on the way. There are generally time limits that have to be observed when you buy insurance for a new vehicle, so don't procrastinate.

Don't drive an uninsured or underinsured vehicle at any time, because anything can happen on the road. The consequences of not having insurance can follow you for years, cost you a fortune, and ruin your credit and finances if you get into an accident.

Underwriters of insurance take a dim view of what they consider total irresponsibility because as they see it, by driving without insurance, you not only are disregarding your own well being, but the safety and care of others.

You could wind up with a destroyed car and still have to pay off the car loan. In addition, the policy that you will buy next will be astronomical beyond your capacity to believe the bill when you see it. Believe me, you don't want to pay the kinds of premiums created when the insurers find out a person had no insurance at the time of a prior accident.

Leasing Versus Buying

You may be offered the opportunity to lease instead of buying a car. You have to know what leasing is and how it can affect your bottom line.

When you lease a car, you choose a term during which you pay for an agreed upon price. Theoretically, the price should be less than it would be if you purchased the car. A residual amount should be subtracted from the price of the car, because you are only using up part of the life of the car, and the dealer will sell it at the end of the lease. The residual amount (expressed as a percentage) varies with make and model. Find out the residual percentage for that particular car. Residual percentages can be vastly different from car to car. Subtract it from the total price you have researched for the car. Divide the remainder by the number of months you are leasing and that should be your lease payment before interest.

Find out how much interest or other money is being tacked on and why. Don't let anyone rush you in understanding the figures. Having a pocket calculator or loan calculator can be useful because unless you are a genius, you will not be able to figure out the right price.

Since you don't own the car and will be bringing it back to the dealership at the end of the term, the dealer has the option of selling their car to make up the money at the end of the lease. There are conditions on leased cars, like the amount of insurance you have to carry, the type of insurance you have to carry, (because they own the car, not you), and most significantly, the number of miles you can drive the car without an up-charge. If you exceed the mileage agreed upon in the contract, you might have to pay a significant per mile charge. If you leased to save money, and exceed the agreed upon mileage, you will ruin your budget. For instance, if you get a new job with a long commute the lease might wind up costing more than you had counted on.

Sometimes, if it is part of the contract, you can purchase the car at the end of the lease, but make sure that you have the entire deal hammered out in the beginning. Lease prices are negotiable just like any other prices, so know the residual, and all the other steps in this book.

Remember that just because the car still belongs to the dealership, it doesn't mean that they pay for the insurance. You have to insure the car at a level agreed upon in the contract.

Lastly, the day will come when you have to bring in the car and once again decide whether you want to buy a car or lease another car. When you buy a car, you have the option of trading it in whenever you are ready. When you lease a car, you have to turn the car back over to the dealer on a certain date.

When you return the car, depending upon your contract, the car might be inspected and if deficiencies are found, you also might be penalized monetarily for those deficiencies depending upon your contract. Read the entire contract before making a decision to lease to make sure the provisions are consumer friendly and meet your needs.

So, when does a lease make sense? It would make sense, for example, for a person who actually does buy a new car every three years, who doesn't use the car a lot, and has an upscale income that can be predicted to continue reliably for several years ahead.

Before you sign any contract, make sure the numbers reflect everything you have talked about in the last few hours. Make sure everything is correct and don't sign anything if you still have questions.

The Keys

Wow! You can't wait to get out of the dealership and drive your new car. In their excitement to leave, most people forget a couple of critical last steps.

❖ **Do you have all the copies of your paperwork?**

You may need facts listed on these pages for your insurance agent. Don't leave the dealership without your copies. If you are applying for a private loan to see if you can obtain a better rate you will need them too.

❖ **Do you know the maintenance schedule required by the manufacturer or insurer to keep your warranties in force?**

If you do not follow the maintenance guidelines for your vehicle, you might find that standard warranties and even extra warranties that you have included as part of your loan are not in force when you need the wonderful things they promised and you bought.

Imagine your horror when an expensive repair that would have been covered under your warranty is turned down and you have to reach into your purse and pull out several unexpected hundreds of dollars. You are saying "but, but" and they are saying that it was all in the paperwork they gave you when you signed up for the warranty. Pay close attention and make sure you get a maintenance schedule related to the requirements of the warranty, read it and understand it. Follow it to the letter.

❖ **Is the tag on your car?**

I can't begin to tell you how easy it is to drive down the street and not even realize that you have no tag on the back of your vehicle. You are already exhausted. Do you want to have to explain this to a vigilant policeman? While you might get in some interesting car talk about the new car, he will likely just go ahead and issue you a ticket for driving without one. His city needs revenue.

Don't depend on the dealership to take care of this significant detail without your participation. The car is sold now and their interest in you is waning. There is a new client in their binoculars and you are disappearing into the ether.

When my husband picked up his truck, he called the insurance agent to add it to our policy. Then he drove it to an agent for the new truck inspection. She walked around the truck and when she reached the back bumper, she asked him if he forgot to put the tag on. Luckily, he was very close to the dealership and was able to go back, get it and attach it before he got a ticket. He could have driven all over town for days and not known.

❖ **Don't leave the dealership parking lot until your salesman goes over the operating features of the car one more time.**

When you have been driving another vehicle for a while, you are used to the controls for the wipers, windshield washer, radio, signal lights, emergency signals, brightness knobs, shifters, and other functions. Before you leave the car lot, insist that someone show you one more time where they are and how they work in this car.

❖ **How many times have you heard someone say that they once wrecked a brand new car?**

You can sympathize that such a weird thing could happen and give them a copy this book, because you know they will at least get a better deal the next time.

Why does this happen so often to good drivers? I once saw a customer (not mine, because I wouldn't let them go without instructions) drive out of the dealership onto a crowded road. She made a left hand turn and thought she was signaling. Instead, she used the windshield cleaner knob. Water shot all over the window as she entered the road. She didn't see another vehicle emerging from across the street right away. They almost collided, but luckily, both got away without injury.

So, please be safe and take the few minutes it takes to have your salesperson go over the important elements of your dashboard before you drive. It can save your new car, your good health, and my peace of mind.

From The Author

I genuinely hope that the information contained in this book will help you to save money, save time, and make your life more comfortable.

All dealerships are not run the same, so you might use all the information, part of it or none of it. It will be a good idea to keep a copy around for reference to use in negotiating for any large purchase over the years.

I am sending you out with an army of women behind you. I hope that you are going to be so good at buying a car that you will have to give away this book to keep from having to go buy cars for your friends, relatives, and acquaintances! I hope this book will increase your abundance in every way and give you a new sense of your own worth, as well as your net worth.

Warmest Regards,
Linda Balk

The Real Deal For Women™

Send your friends for
free newsletters on
Buying Cars!

Visit http://www.realdealforwomen.com often for more information about upcoming books in the series !

©2007 Linda Fleming Balk All Rights Reserved Worldwide

www.ingramcontent.com/pod-product-compliance
Lightning Source LLC
Chambersburg PA
CBHW032010190326
41520CB00007B/416